T0274012

RIGHT
MEDITATION

RIGHT MEDITATION: FIVE STEPS TO REALITY
This is a complete guide to meditation as the art of
spiritual life, from starting to meditate right through to
the final step – entering the truth of life and death in
the living body. This little book is the product of vast
experience and deep knowledge. Read it in a few
hours. Live its teaching for a lifetime.

BARRY LONG was arguably the most radical and
pioneering spiritual teacher of the twentieth century,
though his contribution to contemporary spirituality is
often overlooked. He was the first to introduce to the
western world a teaching of practical self-knowledge
and immense wisdom without reference to eastern or
occult traditions. 'Right Meditation – Five Steps to Reality'
was written just before he died in 2003 and concluded
his life's work.

BARRY LONG

RIGHT MEDITATION

Five Steps to Reality

BARRY LONG BOOKS

Published 2024 by
BARRY LONG BOOKS

'Barry Long Books' is the publishing imprint of
The Barry Long Foundation International
www.barrylongbooks.com
www.barrylong.org

Hardback: ISBN 978 1 899324 50 7

Cataloguing-in-Publication Data:
A catalogue record for this book is available from The British Library.

Cover design: Barbara de Vries, Liselot Jansen
Digitally printed in the UK and the USA

CONTENTS

FOREWORD

Barry Long (1926-2003) was one of the most radical spiritual teachers of the twentieth century. He broke with religious and spiritual traditions to speak directly in straightforward terms to the experience of modern life. But his teaching was nonetheless rooted in the ages-old spiritual discipline and practice of sitting meditation.

Today meditating is widely practised and the word 'meditation' is in common use. This was not so when Barry Long began teaching the art in London in the late 1970s. Students of eastern spirituality and yoga would have come across meditation as sitting in silence or chanting mantras and others may have associated it with Christian contemplation. But there were no popular books dedicated to the art of it and none were written in plain words or stripped of mysticism. Not until Barry Long arrived in London from his native

Australia, via India, with the simple introductory guide he'd written: Meditation A Foundation Course. His idea was to present it to a London publisher. But in those days, far from having any popular appeal, a little book on meditation was too esoteric and oddball to be published commercially. Eventually Barry Long's students published it themselves and in several editions through the 1980s and 1990s it gradually became a standard guide to meditation, was published in several languages and remains in print to this day.

Following on from the Foundation Course, came 'Start Meditating Now' which Barry Long wrote and recorded to be released first on cassette tape and later as a CD and more recently as a download. It has reached thousands over the years and is much commended as one of the best means of entering the inner space of 'the unconscious made conscious'.

This teaching on tape was supported by another recording: 'How to stop thinking - in ten lessons'. And there was another book too, following on from the Foundation Course: 'Stillness Is the Way: An Intensive Course in Meditation'.

Central to all this teaching of meditation is the proposition that the practice must inform every aspect of a spiritual life; and its lessons are to be applied in the ordinary circumstances and struggles of daily living. In the wide-ranging embrace of the whole Barry Long teaching, meditation comes first and last.

So it was that as Barry Long came to the end of his life – when he knew he was dying – he wanted to complete the circle and state the main tenets and practices of his meditation. These are 'The Five Steps', described in a brief manuscript written in 2003. It had been lost and forgotten and only came to light again in 2022. Its value is enduring and is a final testament to the great and often overlooked contribution that Barry Long made to contemporary spirituality.

The Five Steps brings us back to the simple, clear, practical guidance that is the hallmark of Barry Long's timeless teachings. They are so practical and down-to-earth and yet they open up a vast cosmic vista – as you'll discover in this little book. It doesn't take many pages for Barry Long to take us deeply into truth, to the heart of the art of meditation. On the first page of the manuscript, on an otherwise blank page, he had inscribed these words:

'Into the wider scheme of things . . .'

Clive Tempest

INTRODUCTION

Right meditation is an art. Like all disciplines, it begins with practise. And with practise, we trust that the study or activity we give our time to will eventually become easy, effort-free and fulfilling. This is especially so in studying a form of art, art being any activity that subtly delights within.

This is not to suggest that the study of an art form doesn't sometimes cause frustration and impatience. But those reactions are part of the learning process that actually sorts out whether we're serious enough to continue. If we're not, we give up. That doesn't mean you're a failure. It simply means that the study is not right for you just now. But if you're able to persevere, art is its own reward.

Anything can be turned into an art. We see this, albeit on rare occasions these days, when someone has a gift for what they're doing. It may be a mechanic who communicates the sense of being one with the car he's tuning. He has practised, probably felt like kicking the machine at times, but has followed his inner delight – and won through. To be moved in that way is part of men and women's perennial search for fulfilment.

Nevertheless, any art that depends on external objects or activity is secondary to the great art of you making you a more complete, harmonious and intrinsically creative man or woman. This is the function of meditation, a completely inner practice that necessarily, but secondarily, relates to the external world.

The sole purpose of meditation, as you are about to appreciate in reading this book, is to increase the speed of intelligence in that body reading these words. That is not to say your intelligence is inferior. It's not. It is quite capable, with the right inner guidance, of reaching an enormous potential completely beyond the understanding of the worldly surface mind.

PRACTICE IS THE KEY

Each of the Five Steps needs to be practised as you are reminded from within, or by events. Don't wait . . . do it now, then, at that moment – for the moment of being reminded has a helpful power of its own. And don't concentrate on one Step and forget about the others. Practise them all. As you continue you'll be amazed at the positive changes that occur inwardly and out-wardly. No step at any stage is redundant until all have fused together as a complete state of life – which externally becomes a new way of living.

Remember, the Five Steps are part of your whole life – not something separate – and are done at any time of your waking day. When you are busy, practise pausing for a couple of minutes to give time to a Step. Other good times are when you're waiting for a bus, a person, an appointment or during a teabreak. The pauses will make the days easier and you less tired at the end of them.

Everything in this book I'm suggesting you do, I have done by living it. If you sense that I have some wisdom and knowledge beyond the ordinary, then that is possible in time for you too.

I wish you well in this wonderful journey.

STEP ONE

Releasing Your Prisoners

Nearly everyone has emotional prisoners locked in their chest or belly. These are emotional replicas of people you've resented or felt have betrayed or hurt you in the past. You keep them there, unconsciously guarding them, just like a jailer.

When you're reminded of an old resentment, that emotional prisoner comes to life and troubles you. You get a stab in the chest, a band of tightness across the chest, or an ache in the tummy. You then can't meditate or be really still because something's going on in your body that you don't understand. Your prisoners are screaming, 'Free me, free me', but it is human nature to hold tight and not let them go.

These unconscious emotions provoke us to accuse and blame other people and events for our life instead of facing the fact that it is 'my' life and 'I' alone am responsible for it.

What you have to do is consciously practice releasing your prisoners. And remember, some of them are 'institutionalised' and comfortable where they are. They don't want to go. And if they do go they will soon return unless you are vigilant.

Releasing prisoners is not the same as forgiving the people concerned. You wouldn't need to forgive if you hadn't judged. The need to forgive arises from the judging of others. While you continue to judge others you'll be moved at times to grandly forgive them, when really, you're the one causing the emotion with your judging. No matter how much you say you forgive, other prisoners will remain in your chest to trouble you.

This is because human nature has interpreted forgiveness as forgiving a particular person or people. They are identifiable. And that's the error. What you have to practise doing is forgiving all your prisoners, the whole lot, NOW, all at once, without naming. You let them go altogether like a flock of birds. And the reason it works is not because you think you're letting them go, but because you are consciously every moment giving them no place to rest inside you. There are also many forgotten emotional hurts buried in your body that you just can't identify. Trying to identify them doesn't work if you're serious about returning to the state of simplicity or guilessness, which is essential to inner freedom.

The practice of this step is to say, and really mean it within, 'I release everyone I ever thought or felt hurt me, failed me or harmed me. I will have none of this resentment in me.

'I surrender now and every moment this lack of innocence, this judging of others. I will not have it.'

And to the emotions, 'I will have nothing in me against anyone. Be gone from me. I free you in love.'

You have to walk around consciously emptying yourself of resentment towards any person or event. Consciously means, not just reciting the words intellectually, but being there with your intelligence.

Resentment undermines your physical and psychological well-being and helps to spoil the quality of life.

Something else to bear in mind is that while you judge others you will judge yourself and cause self-doubt. Self-doubt is a very troublesome and common emotion among people.

The old saying, 'forgive your enemies' can be misleading if it's not done in the wholehearted and immediate way I've described. If you tell your child at school when he or she is punched and bullied to forgive the one who bullies them, you'll confuse the child. The young can't really forgive; they'll only suppress the emotions and suppression builds up in the body as unhappiness. It's much the same with, 'love your enemies.' You can't love your enemies. But you and your child can be intelligent enough not to hold anything against anyone – while still taking any external practical action you're moved to.

Please know that this meditation is not like any other. As the introduction says, it has unfolded in the author during more than three decades of spiritual teaching. The meditation does not involve visualisation. It is original and non-idealistic and covers the whole human condition as something practical you can always do. At every stage of meditation you have to be practical. You have to see things as they are and not as you or others imagine them. If it's not practical – something you can do – what's the good of it?

So, have you any prisoners in there? Do you think you were betrayed? Do you think you were abused by your mother or father, perhaps sexually abused, and hold on to the thought of it? It's the thought that keeps the painful emotion alive. Endeavour to never think about it and your quality of life will improve. It is human nature – not our real nature – to blame others. In the wider scheme of things all of us are to blame or nobody is to blame. We are the product of two thousand million years of life on earth. Who are you going to blame for all that?

Because the human mind and emotions repair themselves so quickly, you have to be constantly on guard against being resentful – even of past events. It is one thing to walk away from an event that causes difficulties in your life or to see it through (whichever you are moved to do at the time); but it is something else to do this without allowing resentments to take hold, either at the time, or later when you are tempted to look back. This applies particularly to past lovers and past painful events.

The fact is you can't meditate unless you are still. Emotional prisoners inside your belly or chest are going to play up. When someone mentions a name or event alluding to them, the emotions vibrate at the level of the resentment, and you are disturbed. You'll be still at other times, like many people are who don't practise this meditation. But to be still sometimes is like having someone jab you in the back unexpectedly. It's best to know what's untrustworthy and unreliable in your body – and that is your concealed emotions.

The resentments are very, very cunning. They are also very, very quick, very swift and outspeed the surface mind. What we're endeavouring to do, is to heighten the immediacy of your intelligence so that eventually it outspeeds any emotion. Then old resentments cannot come back and new ones cannot enter.

It's a gradual process. You have to practise. And you have to be inwardly moved to practise; otherwise you'll rush through it, gloss over the point, and the practice will be less effective.

So this first step is to stop accusing or blaming others for your life. It's a big step because every time you have an argument, you are in effect disturbed by someone. That means you've taken an emotional position. It is possible, as you know, to talk to people without taking a position; in which case you simply exchange facts. But where emotional issues are involved both parties tend to talk from biased personal impressions more than facts and the communication becomes muddied and often heated. It is best as much as possible for you not to get into accusations or blaming; and to keep to facts. The emotions in the other person may not allow this, in which case it is advisable to conclude civilly and try again another time. Positions create counter-positions.

Spiritual freedom comes down to no longer being a slave to your emotional self.

The human race has been blaming each other and events for its unhappiness and ignorance since time began; and all this has done is cause more unhappiness, self-doubt and lack of love. You have to see this for yourself. I can only point the way.

So, are you holding anything against anyone? Or holding on to any painful events? Don't answer off the cuff.

Pause.

Wait.

Look within.

Be still.

If something is there let it reveal itself – which it will. And release it.

Finally, when your prisoners are freed, so will you be to that extent, and there'll be nothing there – except the reality in Step Two.

STEP TWO

Focusing on Pure Sensation

Most meditation methods start with watching thought and emotions. When you are successfully practising releasing emotional prisoners, you're through that and it's not necessary to watch your thought process. Troublesome or aimless thought is due to stored-up emotions. As the emotions are reduced, so is the thinking.

Step Two follows on naturally after Step One. All it requires is for you to have developed sufficient one-pointedness to focus your attention on the pure sensation in the body.

Your attention is the natural intelligence which enables you to be aware of existence. What you don't focus your intelligence on, you don't see or hear. So there's nothing really difficult about doing this exercise.

You begin by understanding that there are only two realities in the body – pure sensation and intelligence.

These are all that's used. Let us start. After you've read
what to do, close the eyes, focus within, and proceed.

Inside your hands is a vibration, a tingling feeling.
Pause and connect with that now.
The tingling can be subtle to begin with but soon
becomes evident. This is pure sensation, 'pure' mean-
ing it is not caused by any thought, emotion or external
trigger. It's always there.
The same tingling sensation is in your feet.
Right?
Now your nose.
There it is again.
In your chest is the same tingling.
Pure sensation is not the same as emotion which
sometimes rises in the chest as anxiety and thinking.
Pure sensation never varies. Focusing on it requires no
thought. In fact thought distracts the attention and
makes you feel you've 'lost it'. That's not the case,
however. It's always there when you are still enough.

Now, close your eyes and go around the various
parts of the body on your own – including the head,
shoulders, legs, knees, buttocks and small of the back.
One after the other.
Take your time.
Don't gloss.
Pause for several seconds on each part.

Do it consciously.
Be there.

Eventually, after you've practised often enough, the sensation of all the parts will merge into one and the physical body will disappear. Of course it doesn't disappear for others, only for you. While you're fully absorbed in the sensation with your eyes closed, you'll discover that you wouldn't know you had a body. But, due to habit, the mind will always try to recreate the body in the memory, and now and again an arm or a leg will appear in your consciousness. Don't let that distract you. Stay with the sensation, not the image, and the image will evaporate.

You can be in this state of absorption for a considerable time. But you'll notice, as part of the exercise of becoming more conscious, that something invariably happens to bring you out. You'll be made to move or reflect on something; the phone or doorbell will ring. Existence is a place of movement and something always happens to bring you back to the body – eventually.

Pure sensation has nothing in it – no mental activity, no conclusions, no interpretations. It is the reality of the body without the physicality. The sense of having a body actually comes out of pure sensation. Pure sensation is the very origin of the senses, the source of the physical body which creates the world and the earth around us. When your intelligence merges with this sensation you're at the source of your existence. In other words, take away the physical senses, as in death, and the incredible reality of the body still is! But we must be careful not to go into idealism. Until we die, we'll always have a physical body to return to.

Sometimes while you're absorbed you'll sense a thought on the perimeter of the stillness trying to push in. Thought can't cross the stillness unless you give it your attention. So keep focused. Thoughts are like hovering jackals impatient to devour the silence. The silence/stillness is actually pure intelligence. Thought, on the other hand, is an inferior reflective intelligence dependent on the memory. Pure intelligence is direct, immediate, now! Thought is indirect and takes time.

If you do start thinking – and there's little doubt it will happen – don't try to battle with thought; you'll never win.

It is self battling with self.

Start again: open the eyes, see what's immediately in front of you, close the eyes, and go back to focusing on the sensation in the different parts of the body.

By opening the eyes and returning briefly to the outer world, you break the momentum of the thought that's already started. You're then fresh and new again. Eventually your attention drops very quickly into the sensation of the whole of your body. But there are days when this doesn't happen so easily. So your safety net, whenever there's a difficulty, is to start again from the beginning by focusing on the sensation in the different parts.

Also, you have to guard against slipping into a trance before you're really in the stillness. Here again, being with the sensation will keep you conscious or alert; whereas in a trance you lose the presence of the sensation and drift along in a kind of comfortable near-sleep.

You can't think or be emotional when you are focused on pure sensation. However the movement of emotion can be mistaken for pure sensation. The difference is that emotion contains personal feelings whereas pure sensation is utterly impersonal. In short, during absorption in pure sensation the sense of 'I' or any identifying feelings vanish and the two realities of intelligence and sensation merge.

Pure sensation is the state of the embryo before the baby starts to leave the womb. It is the edge of existence. At death from old age or disease, the physicality of the body gradually gives way to pure sensation. Pure sensation is the last thing coming into existence and going out. So, being fully absorbed in pure sensation is the purest state of meditation and a kind of preview of before and after existence.

Stay with the pure sensation and if there is anything to be revealed, that state of intelligence will reveal it.

Don't look for esoteric or psychic happenings you've heard or read about. Discover what is new in your own experience.

The merged state of pure sensation and intelligence – absorption – has enormous virtue and truth. It is the key to the deeper levels of the unlimited psyche which you can access.

All this is a deeper than usual way of looking at things. It takes a lot of intelligence to break the common addiction to scientific rationalism and materialism – and to the notion that there's something out 'here' that's real. Focusing on pure sensation speeds up the intelligence so that false notions, no matter how popularly held, are seen for what they are. It is an extraordinary transformation to be able to see things realistically. It brings a deep sense of relief from tensions stored in the body and from some of the burden of existence. And it begins now, inside the body reading these words.

Before we proceed, repeat the exercise of going around the pure sensation of the body parts with the eyes closed.

Be easy.

Relax.

Stillness is the way.

Don't connect with any feelings in your belly or

chest because that is emotion, false sensation. If the emotions are too strong for you to start focusing on the hands or feet, it's probably best to try again later.

The next important exercise is to practise meditating with the eyes open. You start by meditating with the eyes closed and, when comfortably absorbed, open them. The idea is to remain focused on the pure sensation within and to not be distracted by what you're seeing. This means you refrain from subtly naming anything in front of you. You see it all as a whole, as a scene, without particularising. This does take practice because we're all taught from infancy to recognise and name things and it's become a subconscious habit. In time the practice of absorption will break the habit.

Learning to meditate usually begins with setting aside, say, 30 minutes or so, twice a day for practise. This is very much a beginner's routine which you would have completed long ago by following my earlier publications on meditation. We are much further advanced now and need to see that meditation, finally, can't be a partial thing. It has to be something that can be practised most of the time – and for most of the time in your daily life your eyes are open.

Stating the obvious to make the point, if you walked around meditating with your eyes closed you'd soon bump into something. So we have to learn, by practising, how to meditate consciously while walking down the busy street without being distracted by the passing scene.

Again, the art is to not particularise what you're seeing. You have to let the scene keep changing, as it will, without holding on to any particular aspect.

Of course if something in particular grabs your attention, you'll be momentarily, or for a time, distracted.

But that doesn't matter.

It's the overall practice of disidentification that counts.

You practise letting the passing parade pass without joining in.

Eventually you'll get the idea and it will become easier and easier.

You're not having to invent anything; this is the natural way of detached perception.

To reach this stage it will help to practise staying in your senses while walking down the street. This means simply being aware of the whole scene as presented by the senses without thinking or interpreting what you're seeing. Since you're aware and not thinking, you won't bump into anything and your body will automatically look both ways before crossing the road.

The mind names objects because it works off the five senses of sight, sound, taste, smell and touch-feeling. The five senses are differentiated – not connected in themselves. Connecting them up so that our perception of the world 'makes sense', is the mind's job. But as each sense is reporting a different sensation, our impression would be quite disjointed except for the amazing speed of the ego behind the mind.

Here you need to understand the difference between the surface mind which names objects and the ego. The surface mind is completely dependent on the ego, but doesn't know it. The mind thinks it's the only intelligence in the body. But really it's a limping reflection of the intelligence of the ego. The ego, in spite of common misconceptions, is the innate intelligence of the body, the instinct the body is born with. You know from your own experience that instinct is infinitely faster than the mind, as demonstrated when you touch a hotplate and the body withdraws instantly before the mind can work out what's happening.

The ego is continuously and sleeplessly poised and alert for any sign through the senses of a threat to the survival or normal functioning of the body. In the event of an unusual smell of smoke, the ego alerts the surface mind and sends it searching for a confirming sign in one of the other external senses. The mind checks the sense of sound by listening intensely for the crackle of fire, or the sense of sight for a sign of flames, and so on. Because each sense is independent of the others, the mind has to go from one sense to the other for confirmation – and this 'slowness' introduces the sense of time we're all familiar with. The ego is of an infinitely swifter time. The ego works through the nervous system and its speed is comparable with electricity which approaches the speed of light. The mind, working through the memory and emotions, lumbers along at the comparable speed of sound.

What we're endeavouring to do is reduce our identification with the surface mind so that our intelligence is more in line with the swiftness of the ego – a time beyond.

The mind's habitual switching from sense to sense gives an unreliable picture of what's happening in the external world. So much so that if we're honest we seldom know what's really going on out 'there'. The continuous mental activity keeps the mind subconsciously busy, apart from, as we all know, constantly referring as thought to the unreliable memory for confirmation of what is happening. Changing over to be more in tune with the intelligence of the body gives an inner perception of the outer that eliminates much, if not all, the confusion and mis-identification.

The big question for you to look at now is whether you actually have a complete physical body as the senses and mind imply. And as a corollary, whether the intelligence I refer to as the ego or instinct is in fact the amazing intelligence implicit in pure sensation. And then, whether it is the genius of pure sensation creating in the lesser medium of sense the whole fantastic impression of a sensory body, world and life.

In what follows, let us examine the validity of the senses. You do this by examining each point made in your own experience. This means in the moment of reading. If it's not true in your own experience, it's not true for you – or you haven't looked closely enough at the fact.

Each sense gives a separate impression of the body and the world, but not one of them gives a total view. Neither can the mind present a complete picture – although it tries by filling in the blanks with imagination. You can't see the back of your body while you're seeing your toes; you never see your face direct: your impression is dependent on a mirror – an actual mirror or the mirror of the unreliable memory.

The fact is that no one can show you with your senses a complete physical body; because there's no such thing. The physical body is a sensory impression held together in the mind, by the mind. Its only reality is in pure sensation – behind the mind and the divided and partial senses.

So now, focus once again on the pure sensation with eyes closed, then open them and witness the scene in front of you without thought or naming.

The value of this, as mentioned, is to interrupt and finally break the mind's habitual momentum that, despite every effort to stop, expresses itself very painfully in sleepless nights of worry. Interrupting the unconscious continuity of the mind also helps to eliminate aimless thinking which, when intensified by emotional disturbance, turns into worry and anguish.

In walking around and witnessing the scene without interpretation, you are preparing for an extraordinary potential revelation in consciousness. This is, that in a profound level of the inner psyche, far behind the divided physical senses, is the unified sense centre, which I call the 'nucleate' sense centre. This is the very origin of physical/material existence.

The nucleate sense centre is in the radiant depths of the inner psyche close to where the psyche adjoins spirit, source of all. The human brain, being an instrument of separation, divides the incoming radiance into the five physical senses. To the brain the senses must always remain differentiated, but in consciousness able to resonate at the speed of the radiance, the truth behind the physical senses is revealed.

STEP THREE

Gratitude and Devotion

Combined with the practice of Step One and Step Two, nothing enhances the intelligence more than gratitude. We all express gratitude to those who help us in need. But that's not the gratitude I'm speaking of. What I'm referring to is gratitude to the Source of all the good in your life. That source of course is not any person. It's the source behind the person, the source of your life.

Human nature most of the time concentrates on trying to solve problems and difficulties. You're already engaged in a different approach by first releasing your emotional prisoners which cause many of the problems and difficulties; and then by focusing on the pure sensation in the body. Absorption in pure sensation increasingly demonstrates that there is something greater than the physical body behind the body. In other words, a source. And in time it becomes clearer, that there's a source behind each source, which continues until you reach an intimation of eternity or God.

I'm not asking you to believe anything in advance. I'm simply saying what you will discover in your own experience if you continue to be serious in the practise of this meditation. Perhaps you've already experienced what I'm saying.

You begin Step Three by inwardly, and perhaps vocally while alone, giving thanks for the good in your life.

Be specific.

Everyone has good in their life.

What's good in yours?

Name it.

Give thanks for it.

The more you specify, the more you'll find you are thankful for.

Do you have a roof over your head? Warmth? A couple of meals a day? Someone, or something to love such as dog, cat or bird? Do you have a largely untroubled life compared to so many around you? Are you fortunate?

The answer of course is that you are fortunate – once you start appreciating what you have and not dwelling on what you think you want.

Eventually, you'll be a walking-but-not-necessarily-talking 'thank you'. You won't need to be so specific except in the moment when gratitude for something arises in you and you simply say, 'thank you, thank you.'

The thing you're being thankful for is one with that moment so you don't have to be vocally specific.

We're talking of an intelligence behind even the moment of events – the supreme intelligence of the source of all.

Remember, you're not thanking anyone or anything in particular.

You are thanking the invisible source of everything.

See that there is much more good in your life than what's not so good.

Everything in physical existence must repeat the pattern of the greater reality behind it. This means that life on earth basically must follow the patterns in the psyche (as the psyche must follow spirit). Gratitude, being an inner expression, originates in the psyche and as we've seen is fundamentally love of the source. In our physical medium of separate bodies, gratitude continues to be vital to love – especially in the all-important love-relationships between man and woman.

Gratitude in love-relationships scales down to acknowledgement. If you wish to keep a loving relationship vital and fresh, you need to practise acknowledging the good things that you see in your partner. You acknowledge these things in the moment as often as you see them. This helps to keep your love of the other alive and fresh instead of gradually falling into the normal physical pattern of taking love for granted; of assuming that the other knows you love them without your having to consistently demonstrate your awareness of why you love them.

You must have seen this deterioration happen in your own love-life as well as in the relationships of others. Lovers start off mouthing wonderful things to each other but over time the frequency diminishes until finally, and to me tragically, the relationship becomes for the most part habitual and stale.

In the moment of seeing a loving or simple twinkle in the eyes of the other, you acknowledge how attractive or pleasing it is to you. You acknowledge the smile or lightness in the face that you used to love and still love when you see it. The little gestures of kindness or goodness towards others you acknowledge; also the care that the other takes to look attractive for you; and the many many things that made you simply love to be with them in the first place. And always acknowledging in the moment of seeing; not harking back to the past or uttering those terrible words 'of course I love you', as justification for your lack of vital love and aliveness.

Once the inclination to find the truth is awakened within, as has happened for you to be reading this, it helps to know that there is a wider scheme of things behind the material world. And you don't have to depend on what I'm saying because a certain sense of the scheme is already inside you as innate self-knowledge.

This is due to the fact that everything that happens in existence is already planned in the deeper levels of your own psyche. The plan is not fatalistic, meaning pre-determined as the mind might think, because existence occurs in a very slow time compared with the inner regions. The plan in the inner regions is fluctuating every moment but in earth time the changes are virtually imperceptible and give an impression of an almost unchanging continuity.

However, things do change as we all know. But mostly we only notice the changes when we interpret them as good or bad. For example, someone close dies. That's a big change. But when someone close goes on living it's just another part of the 'unchanging' scene. Same thing when there's no interruption to your job or income. But change is inevitable, isn't it? It's just that we tend to drift along pretty unconsciously until change comes, or hits us.

Perhaps in the past you've been like the scientist and thought that you and existence have no intelligent source. That it all just happened and then evolved, with no plan, no scheme, no purpose and perhaps that there is not even an intelligence behind it equal to the inferior intelligence of the scientist himself – who nevertheless takes great care to plan his experiments in advance? Why does the scientist and everyone plan? Because the constant unfolding of life in existence must, by spiritual imperative, repeat in the psyche and then our lower octave, the defining pattern of the divine source of intelligence behind it. Which, in this case, is what manifests as planning.

Today science is diligently working at creating artificial intelligence instead of working on the vestigial intelligence the scientist himself already has. Robots will never be really intelligent. It takes a robot to build a robot – and a great deal of planning.

Every moment of emerging existence is perfectly planned. When I look at the sea, I say to Sara my partner, 'Every wave accounted for. Every bubble accounted for.' But to see this takes extraordinary gratitude and devotion to the source – which is possible for everyone in time. But such things can only be seen in the moment – every moment being the much spoken of 'moment of truth'. Moments can't be held on to and thought about. Once seen, the reality of a moment is realised – made real – and any reflection by the mind is unnecessary.

Do you assume your birth is not accounted for? That your death is not already accounted for? Do you think both just happen, that you can walk in front of a car with no purpose involved? That's how scientific materialism thinks. It's true that one thing follows another in the evolving sensory world, but intelligence does not evolve. Intelligence is always here, in every body. What prevents it from operating at full capacity are the innumerable short circuits in the human system beginning with having a flesh and blood brain. Added to this are our self-generated feelings and emotional attachment to transient objects, as well as the habit of mistaking attachment for love.

These and the many other aspects of our ignorance reduce the original intelligence down to the human condition – which is the cause of all the wars, all the divorces, all the single mothers and fathers. You only have to see this, not try to do anything to change it outside of changing yourself. Seeing things as they are is a sign of increasing intelligence.

Another reason it's so difficult for humanity to be intelligent is that the media is our main source of information. The media's focus is on conflict and scandal rather than on the good in the life of the journalist writing the stuff. This tends to influence and feed our interests in external matters so that the inner world beyond emotions is commonly ignored.

Immediately inside your physical body is the psyche. The psyche is where you think, dream and plan. You then try to implement your plans in the gross physical world, but they seldom turn out as you saw them in the swifter time of the psyche. You've experienced this. It's not just because I told you. You are totally familiar with planning in the psyche and how rarely it works out as you saw it.

The psyche has many levels of higher intelligence or swifter time until it reaches eternity, where time ends. Beyond eternity is spirit about which nothing much can be said except that spirit is the magnet drawing you and I and all things back towards itself, reality. Thus the divinely predestined movement of consciousness away from existence, as demonstrated by the certainty of physical death, ends temporarily in one of the levels of the psyche.

The counter-magnet to this, also divinely devised, is the degree of attachment to earth experience remaining in the consciousness – which will cause recurrence in a new physical body. The cycle from living, to death, to life, to recurrence, continues until all attachment is dissolved through many living lives. As attachment is reduced by living, the consciousness gravitates to deeper timeless and formless levels of the psyche approaching spirit. Spirit of course is Absolute God – absolute meaning perfect, free from time, imperfection or qualification. Ultimate God, to us, when realised, is the inexpressible wonder of the profound psyche – ultimate meaning farthest or last before perfection.

In the wider scheme of things able to be expressed, the order is: spirit, psyche, physical world – with the Will of spirit being done throughout.

In being grateful for the good in your life you are

acknowledging spirit, the giver of all good, through the psyche. This helps to purify the mind and emotions and makes the swifter intelligence of the psyche more available in your daily life.

DEVOTION

Devotion is a higher spiritual octave that follows on naturally from the fervent practice of gratitude for the good in your life. Characterised by a consuming love of source or God, devotion is an image-free autonomous inspiration ceaselessly informing and purifying the subconscious without any reminder from the senses or surface mind – although frequently rising to mind level and causing an inner smile or joy.

The love of God, the indescribable invisible power, originates in the timeless spirit, and after pervading the increasing time-levels of the psyche, enters the physical through the flesh and blood brain. Here in the spiritual life, although the greatest love of all is of God, the source, it in no way detracts from the love of another living being. In fact, when the love of another is deep enough the invisible God is 'seen' through the person they and we all are.

At its strongest, maternal love – as demonstrated instinctively in all the species – is the natural consuming love of God. In the wider scheme of things it originates from the mythic perception of God, as the earth, being mother of all; and God, as the sun, being father of all. Together, earth and sun produce life on earth.

Religious devotion such as being a devotee of Jesus, the Hindu god Krishna, Buddha or Mohammed is clearly not the devotion I'm speaking of since it puts a concept, an historical figure or idea, between the devotee and the source. This is understandable as a means by which the mind can relate to the invisible God. But the source, God, has no history, no past and is simply the eternal mystery it must always remain inside each one of us. There's no doubt that behind true devotion to religious concepts is a recognition of the source. But the question is, is it possible to love the source direct without in-between images? To me it is.

True devotion is an impersonal divine activity that persists like the heartbeat and breathing without reference to memory or personal choice.

Ceremonial worship, as practised in organised religion, is a choice of the person. The choices available vary widely from religion to religion and the person selects the one closest to their personal beliefs. All ceremonial worship is external, repeating with the body in some way what has been laid down as ritual in the past. But the devotion I'm speaking of is an inner activity of intelligence – not of belief or ceremony –

which I'm now going to ask you to look at in your own experience.

To continue reading this book you have to have a love of something greater than yourself. The subject of the book could hardly be called entertaining or among the interests of most people. Its appeal lies elsewhere within, at a deeper level than the surface mind. That level is the level of true love – true love being an impersonal inclination that defies explanation. 'I simply love it', is probably the only thing that can be said. And that is the love of something greater than yourself.

As part of this continuing exercise I'd like you to see whether that is true or not in your experience.

First, what made you pick up this book? You'd be surprised how many people have written saying that one of my books actually fell out of a library shelf in front of them; or how their hand seemed to automatically go to one. I'm not suggesting this happened to you, but there has to be a starting point for your interest in this subject, as well as to how you happened to come by this book. The point is that what motivated you is a love of something inexplicable and beyond the visible. The exercise is for you to see this; to see that something within has guided you and directed your interest in this direction perhaps for years – despite periods of interruption.

What is that something? In answering you must be careful not to implicate psychic phenomena, 'spirit guides' or that sort of thing. This whole meditation is about you, your deeper reality, and only you. So what is this deeper reality you are that somehow, from behind the scenes, directs the course of your life – frequently in spite of all the personal actions and choices?

It is your self-knowledge. Self-knowledge is the result of innumerable recurrences of living and dying in a mortal physical body. The mortal part of you – your memories, emotions and reflective mind – dies, never to be seen again. But the life – your deeper reality that animates and sustains your mortal body – continues in the psyche and carries with it, or in it, the self-knowledge accruing from that living life. The self-knowledge then joins the store of knowledge of all lives. The process is completely unconscious and autonomous – the miracle of never-ending life repeating the divine pattern of the never-ending God or Self.

Due to self-knowledge, some people have a greater love than others of the invisible God. But you the reader are demonstrating this love. The question is whether you are conscious of it, whether you've yet developed the swiftness of intelligence to separate the invisible impersonal love from your personal loves?

That covers the love part of devotion. But what about the activity necessary for true devotion?

By now you know you have this subtle and inde-finable love inside you. You don't know what it is you're loving but you have the immediate knowledge that the love is there. So here is what you do next.

Without vocalising, without speaking a word, mutely offer within, 'I love you' . . . over and over. Then perhaps, 'I love you. Thank you. I love you. Thank you.'

At first you may have to say the words, and it may seem a bit trite as though you're pretending. But that's not true. The love is there. The love is so subtle the mind and emotions have habitually overlooked acknowledging it. It's not unlike the need to contin-ually acknowledge someone you love, as mentioned earlier. The mind takes the love for granted and finds the utterance of it a bit uncomfortable or 'unneces-sary', not realising that the sustenance of all vital or true love depends on continual conscious or intelli-gent acknowledgment.

Now close the eyes and practise what you've read. Avoid going into a meditative stance or trance. Relax. Be easy.

At first, when not using words or the tongue to give thanks, you are likely to use your throat as a way of mouthing the words without using the tongue. I under-stand that and it's alright because that's the first thing that happens. When you don't open your mouth and don't use the tongue to speak, the throat moves autonomously. Eventually there'll be simply the inner unconscious activity of, 'I love you (or Thee). Thank you. I love you. Thank you. I don't know who you are. I don't know what you are. I don't care. I just love you.'

In the love of God or source there's no object to love. So no personal choice or action is involved. This means that at the deeper level of devotion I'm speaking of, the usual utterance of words is superseded. What can this extremely rare state or place be described as so as to make sense? It is activity, a continuous on-going subconscious activity, which follows on naturally from being truly grateful. Bear in mind that activity is not the same as action. Action is personal and disjointed; activity is general and inevitable.

If you look around you at this moment (and this is part of the exercise of realising devotion) you'll see that there is an infinite amount of ceaseless activity going on behind all the personal actions. Time is passing, leaves are moving, the heart is beating, breathing continues, noises and traffic don't stop, insects and birds sing, human voices seldom are not heard, people are constantly coming and going, the starry heavens keep turning, and life and death go on unimpeded by personal choices and actions.

True devotion is part of this ceaseless impersonal activity and as such is pure unadulterated worship of the mystery of God.

Finally, the whole of what appears to be the body will be resonating with the sense of this divine love without words or contraction in the throat, a complete inner activity of extraordinary intelligence beyond any personal involvement. And there is no priest or image between you and your love. For what you are loving is the unnameable mystery called God, your own being, or Self.

After a time your body might be saying, 'Love. Love. Love.' It might even say, 'Wonder. Wonder. Beauty. Beauty.' For these are all words of true devotion to that which cannot be described.

However, devotion is only in your experience. Someone else can talk about it, but that's not your experience. Your experience is first-hand, now, in the moment. It is yours and yours alone. If someone should say they've experienced it, it's still not your experience.

Such devotion will make you more intelligent, purify you. In whatever you do you'll be of more assistance to others without trying.

Don't tire of offering devotion. And don't think you're just acting it out. You acted out your whole emotional life without noticing, and in the process became attached to your troublesome self. What we're practising is detachment, the reverse process. So you may notice doing it to begin with. But one day you'll say, 'My God, I'm not acting; this is it. I truly love this that is unnameable inside me.'

Now, close the eyes and start meditating, going round the body parts if you have to.

And remember, if you start thinking, open the eyes, pause momentarily, and start again.

Then, while in meditation enter the state of gratitude and thankfulness.

Do this now.

Then open your eyes again and note that the state of gratitude and thankfulness remains as long as you don't think.

The senses themselves don't interfere. It's the mind that interprets what the senses are seeing or hearing and then reacts. That keeps the mind busy, which means you are unable to be really grateful or thankful.

It's essential to be easy, because when you love something like this, when you're truly devotional, you are easy; you can't help it.

There's nothing like love to make one easy.

And there's certainly nothing like devotion to put one in a constant state of loving activity within.

The more you love in this way the more you can be loving in the world. But without loving the unname-able first, loving in the world won't last since the love's not coming from the right source. The source is your source, my source, the source of the whole wide earth and world. If you get too busy in the world with your mind or emotions, you'll forget. Nevertheless when tragedy strikes, the first thing you'll say is, 'God help me.' But by then, if you're acknowledging God as a continuous state of activity within, God will be helping you every moment and you'll know it.

Your love of the unnameable is closer than breathing. It is the source of the love of your child or partner. Without it you will know frustration, disappointment and disenchantment – or the terrible pain of separation when the loved one departs or dies, as all must. When you love the source of love within you first, problems tend to disappear. Your life becomes harmonious; not just in one aspect, but all aspects, for harmony is the essence of the source of all.

That concludes Step Three.

STEP FOUR

Realising Life

Life is the power behind existence and the closest reality to us. If we were not alive, that is, were not life in the form of a flesh and blood brain, we'd have no senses and no physical body – and there would be no existence as we know it. There would not even be the sense of pure sensation to focus on.

Perhaps our brain and existence has an ethereal form behind the physical. But we don't know that in our experience and in this practical meditation we must as much as possible avoid speculation and assumptions.

As all living things die as soon as life withdraws, it is immediately clear that life is the power animating your body at this moment. If you've ever seen a dead human body it's obvious the body is dead, that the amazing quality of life has gone out of it.

A helpful exercise for you, and for any child who enquires about death or life, is to say to the child something like, 'Come into the garden and we'll have a look at some dead beetles and things and see what we can discover.' A conversation like this might follow: 'Look at that dried-up insect or leaf there. What's happened to it?'

'It's dead.'

'That's right. Why is it dead?'

'There's no life in it.'

'Absolutely right. Now, come along, I want you to see your dead grandmother.'

'Oh. They said I shouldn't see her. They say it's too morbid for me.'

'Come with me and I'll make you more intelligent than morbid. There's your dead grandmother. Why is she dead?'

'Well, you can see she's dead. You can see she's dead, can't you?'

'Yes, I can see she's dead; I can see that. But why is she dead?'

'There's no life in her.'

'Right again. Most people who see a dead body don't see that - so perhaps you're a genius. When something is dead it's as plain as the nose on your face, isn't it? Something absolutely vital and essential has withdrawn.'

Let us look at this life thing together and really appreciate how intimate it is to you. This is a necessary exercise because most of humanity takes life for granted, as though eating and sleeping were keeping them alive. You have to be intelligent enough to really see the simple fact that there is something animating the body that can't be explained conceptually except to say it is life.

So let's get closer to life by examining your own immediate experience of it. As always we must do this actually and not just mentally or intellectually. Actually means going still and looking at the fact; in this case looking within at the fact in your own experience now.

What's keeping your body from falling over as you read this? The life in it. In a fainting attack your body collapses like a pack of cards. That's a temporary withdrawal of some of the vitality (an aspect of life) but not of life itself. When life itself withdraws, not only is your body immediately lifeless, but you, the awareness that knew you were alive, vanishes permanently. Let's examine that, too.

How do you know you're alive now? You know because your awareness reflects on your body – on your memory, your feelings, and on what your senses are perceiving – all of which are the effects of having a physical body. What about the life that animates and sustains the body? Even the dictionary definition of life implies a recognition of life's independence of the physical: 'the quality that distinguishes a vital and functional being from a dead body'.

Let's look at the options. Are we, like the scientist, happy to concentrate our energies on intellectually investigating external physical effects (all of which end in death) while ignoring a meaningful investigation of the source of our own being? As ordinary people, are we supposed to blithely get on with our busy living life of mortgages and relationships, without having the time or intelligence to address the life making the living possible?

In your case of course the answer is no. You are giving it the time and necessary effort to overcome the usual human resistance to taking responsibility for the inner life. But this is very difficult for most people. Invariably they look outside themselves at the forms of life instead of addressing the life within. Even respected nature programmes on TV refer to 'life on earth', when the whole content is about forms of life on earth, not life itself.

It seems that everyone we look to for guidance, doesn't know where to look for life, where to start. So how do I identify something in my body so subtly 'me', but seemingly beyond intellectual comprehension?

You connect with the well-being in the body. This is something finely sensational like a sense of the goodness of being alive, or the immediate knowledge or awareness that 'life is good'. Well-being is the first sign of life in every living thing. As we humans are reflective creatures, we can reflect on our well-being, whereas the rest of the species, being wholly instinctive, doesn't have this capability, or need it. They are natural. The human body is also natural but we've imposed on it a sophisticated or clever self. As the dictionary says, sophistication is 'to deprive of genuineness, naturalness or simplicity'. We're endeavouring here to return to our natural simplicity.

Some people to start with have trouble connecting consciously with their well-being. But everyone from time to time is subconsciously in touch with it. Well-being, like life, is so familiar to us that we don't notice it most of the time. When we do we often remark on what a lovely day it is, or how well we feel. Conscious sensitivity is developed through stillness and practice. And it's worth noting that the word well-being implies a 'well of being'.

Say your son or daughter asked this question, 'Tell me Mum or Dad, what's the difference between life and living that I hear you talking about?' What would you reply?

You could say something like this: 'Living is when you have to go to school to learn things, when you trip over and hurt your leg; living is all the things that happen to you and much of living is difficult. Living depends on you having a physical body which gets old and sick and one day is going to die. Your body can't be real because anything that's real can't die. And as you can't live without a body, living also can't be real because it ends with the death of the body.

'Living is what you're not; life is what you are.

'The life you are can never die. It's inside your body now and is what enables your body to walk and breathe. As soon as life withdraws the body dies.'

'But how can I see for myself what life is? You might be just using a word. What is it?'

'Life is the well-being in your body, when you say you feel good. Life or well-being is nourishing your body and mine every moment. Everyone has well-being because everyone has life.

'We lose sight of the well-being of life due to the stresses of living.'

You can't fail in this exercise because once again you're not trying to invent or create something. Well-being is the natural state of a normally healthy body and is reflected in the repose and contentment of all the species, including ourselves. So most of the day when you are not worried, stressed or excited, you have the possibility of registering the 'well of being'. Even when you are ill and well-being seems absent, it is still possible to connect with its source, life in the body.

The sense of well-being is why it's possible for so many people to head off to the football on Saturday afternoon, or for others to glue themselves to the television. They don't have any sickness to distract them from the main event - which is looking out through the senses and being entertained.

Pause now and go still.

Focus on the well-being in your body.

Well-being is so completely positive that it's usually referred to in negative terms – when you don't feel well! It may be that at first all you register is pure sensation. But pure sensation leads to the sense of well-being. All you have to do is keep practising. Pure sensation is actually the subtle rising of the 'well of being'. And remember, when you are consciously in the enjoyment (enjoinment) of well-being that this is the sensational effect of immortal life – the impersonal universal power in every living thing.

So now, put the book down, go still and focus on the well-being in your body.

The next exercise is for you to see in your own experience that there is only one life – seemingly divided by the appearance of innumerable life-forms. I know it's a New Age thing to glibly say we are all one. But we're not all one until the one life has been consciously realised. Life, the most subtle of all subtleties, is the only unity. Life in you is the same as the life in me. The same life is in the grass, the insects, the microbes. The whole earth throbs with the one life. And the realisation of it begins in you.

You begin to really appreciate the one life by relating to it firsthand inside your own body. As you've seen, life is not your body; life animates your body from within. Your body really is just another form of life, albeit the initial form that enables all the other forms of life to be sensed.

The point is for you to be able to see now that there is only one life on earth and that it is in your body, no one else's. Isn't it the same life in another? Oh yes, that's the inevitable intellectual assumption. But it's not actual. The only actuality is that which is in your experience. Being inside someone else's body is not in your experience. For example, no one can tell you what pineapple tastes like; you have to taste a pineapple in your own experience, in your own body. This applies to all aspects of our living life.

But being mostly intellectual creatures we communicate from our experience without knowing whether the other person has experienced what we're talking about. We assume they have. And this results in the vast area of misunderstandings and dissension among people and nations. Take love. When you speak of love to another, is their experience of love the same as yours? If love was just sexual it probably would be. But love, when not just sexual, is different in most people's experience.

The next exercise in realising life concerns beauty. This is because life is beauty and beauty is life. The more you see beauty reflected in the life around you, the more life and therefore beauty is in you. The beauty you see around you is a mirror of how you are inside. But you can't just accept that intellectually; it has to be made real by you seeing more and more beauty, more of life as it is, the purity of life within each form.

Mostly we see the beauty of the forms of life – the creatures and plants – not realising that it is life that gives them their beauty. And particularly, if you look into the eyes of an animal and see the sublime innocence there, you are looking at life's purity. The unprovoked animal doesn't have intentions like we have, doesn't have a hidden agenda. It's just what it is – and it's so refreshing to see what something is rather than what something says it is, or what something wants to be.

And now I must go one step further and say that in seeing beauty in nature or any living thing, what you're really perceiving is the sublime brilliance of the supreme creator, God, shining through the divine medium of life.

Nevertheless, you can't see your own beauty without introducing vanity – beauty doesn't work that way.

Finally, we have to be real enough to see that only life is precious, not the forms of life. If life-forms, which include our bodies, were really precious, they would endure like life itself and not die. Implicit in such a real-isation is the knowledge that prevents the unnecessary harming or killing of any life-form, balanced by the fact that each life-form, including yours and mine, must do as it does until it doesn't – another apparent mystery that stillness eventually resolves.

So now, be still, close your eyes and see that the life in you is keeping your heart beating.

See that your mind and self have no control over how long it will keep beating.

We exercise physically and eat 'healthy' foods to keep fit but even the seemingly 'healthiest' sometimes die suddenly of a heart attack. Is it the failure of the heart that kills? Or is it simply the sudden withdrawal of life?

Then there are the numerous other diseases that 'cause' death over periods of time. Are these really killing the body? Or are they just an appearance of the cause in the appearance of the body, similar to how the invisible winter season can create the appearance of a dead tree or shrub. When the season of life is gradually withdrawing, the body slowly dies.

The consciousness that sees all this can never die.

STEP FIVE

The Solar Plexus

Only the cosmos, the universe, is vast enough, deep enough and profound enough to represent the mystery behind the reality of the apparent physical body. Even so, the universe we see and know and of which our body is the most intimate part, is purely a sensory representation of the reality – the result of having a flesh and blood brain. Yet, because everything to exist must have a greater reality behind it, we can actually look into our physical body and discover a place where the physical universe meets the abstract reality behind it. That place is the solar plexus.

Of course, a considerable stillness of being is necessary. But as you practise this method of meditation as a whole from the first published instructions to these steps, sufficient stillness will have accrued. As a demonstration of this I will later quote a couple of letters from different people describing entry into the cosmic state of solar plexus.

By now you'll have appreciated that the popular notion of meditation and its purpose falls far short of the spiritual art of meditation. Spiritual of course means something out of the ordinary and it is that unusual refinement of sensitivity these steps aim to impart.

Meditation, as I've said, is supposed to make you more intelligent, to give greater discernment in relationships, and to culminate in the realisation of the truth behind existence itself – God, Source or Self. But the outcomes of meditation methods we see around us don't give much indication of something as precious as God-realisation having been attained. In Tibet and other places Buddhist monks meditate all their lives. If you have to meditate all your life, you've got the wrong method; and you've become attached to the method itself. Right meditation is always moving on – moving on towards the practice of the indefinable. Indefinable means beyond words but not beyond communication. In self-knowledge – the rarest subject on earth – inferior words are used to communicate the superior idea; and getting the idea depends on the swiftness of the listener's intelligence. This is where we are now in approaching the solar plexus.

So let us begin. As always, I urge you to examine the

key word for the essential clue. The solar plexus is an extremely sensitive area of radiating nerve fibres in the pit of the stomach behind the small hollow at the base of the breastplate. In Dutch it's called the plexus solaris, in German, sonnengeflecht. And I suspect every language has a name for it relating to the sun, the centre of our cosmic system. You may recall discovering the sensitivity of the solar plexus when as a child someone poked you there and you instantly lost your breath.

As an introduction to this exercise you have to have sufficient swiftness of intelligence to range backwards and forwards seamlessly between the fact of the solar plexus in your body and the outer structure of the solar system as we know it. The solar system is revealed to us, not by the scientists or cosmologists, but by our brain and senses whose source also is the greater reality. Coming from the simplicity of the reality, the solar system is precisely what we all see with our senses without having to indulge in sophisticated scientific speculation.

So now, let us begin with how you and I see the universe.

First there is our physical body. Then there is the earth. Next is the moon. Then the lights and shapes representing the planets. Then, much further out, the sun. Everything beneath the sun is in the solar system. And in the physical body, the solar system is represented by the solar plexus.

The solar system, being a product of the senses, is not real. However, it is provided as a means for us to intelligently approach the reality without the usual interpretations and conclusions of the thoughtful mind. We simply look and see things as they are.

So how, in the actuality of the solar system, can this meditation's emphasis on swifter intelligence be demonstrated as the way to freedom?

Space travel shows that an object has to exceed a speed of around 25,000 miles per hour (40,000 kilometres per hour) to escape the gravitational pull of the earth. Translating this into intelligent perception, it's clear that the first obstacle to spiritual freedom is attachment to the earth. As attachment decreases due to having lived many, many times and seen the futility of the baggage of attachment, the intelligence speeds up until (in the jargon of space travel) escape velocity is reached.

At death of the physical body the main baggage of attachment is discarded; and the consciousness soars into lunar space – the inner space between earth and moon. Compared to the physical, lunar space represents the refined but still lower levels of the psyche, with each being gravitating to a level matching its freedom from attachment. There the being sojourns temporarily in its heaven. But inevitably, attachment to earth experience begins to assert itself and the being of intelligence (or self-knowledge) is born into a new physical body. There it will again gather personal baggage and be weighed down temporarily by attachment until death once more intervenes. This process continues from living life to living life until the orbit of the moon is exceeded.

The crossover from lunar space to planetary space is a climacteric and represents the entry into the beginning of solar space. Solar space consists of increasingly finer levels of the psyche until planetary space itself is exceeded. The being entering those rarified levels is then pure intelligence freed of all attachment to existence. Nothing more can be said about it except perhaps that it is close to merging with God or spirit.

The whole cosmic scheme is present in everybody now. Everybody although 'on earth' now, is at the same time 'somewhere else' in the scheme as self-knowledge or intelligence. That self-knowledge is what is called the 'alter ego' or literally, 'second self.' It guides each of us through the maze of personal involvement and consequences towards the greater good of God and the whole.

Now back to the solar plexus. To go beyond the moon you need sufficient stillness or swiftness to enter the solar plexus. But you can't know this stillness. You can't say whether you're still enough or not still enough. It's beyond the knowing mind. What you do is simply focus on the solar plexus as often as you are able, and when the time is right, or you are, it will reveal some of its mystery to you. Also, bear in mind that everybody is far more self-knowledgeable than can be known with the mind. That's why on occasions when someone asks you a question related to truth, you're amazed at the knowledge expressed in your answer. The impression is you're listening to yourself – and you are: you're listening to your self-knowledge rising from the depths.

Now familiarise yourself with the place of the solar plexus, bearing in mind that there is nothing as subtle in the whole body. In fact, compared with anything else, the solar plexus is as nothing. So you're not endeavouring to sense the sensation anymore, or well-being. You've passed through those and are now focusing direct on the solar plexus. As nothing exceptional is happening, don't assume you're not doing it. The doing, the focusing, is what counts.

At these times the mind or self looks for something exceptional. But the exceptional happens only when self is quiet and still, or absent. Any revelations come from the state itself, which – keep in mind – is the equivalent of nothing. 'Looking for something' introduces an unhelpful sense of self. Also, focusing on the solar plexus doesn't mean that you don't meditate in the usual way – practising each step as you are moved.

At this point I'm going to give you the finest exercise I can express in words. It requires an inner 'doing' that may be mistaken for visualisation. Visualisation may be of some value in the very early days of meditation by making the mind visualise imagined objects instead of meandering aimlessly in its usual undisciplined way. Visualisation may give a passing sense of being in control of the mind. But since it requires you to imagine something that's not already there, visualisation has no place in the spiritual art of meditation. What I'm about to ask you to focus on, is already there. That's why it's real, and why the process works.

The solar plexus is the cosmic prototype or model on which every cell in the physical body is patterned. Cosmically speaking, the solar plexus is the source of life itself in the body, the crossover point between the mystery of life (nothing that can be described) and the phenomenon (everything that can be described).

The solar plexus is primal, which means on the edge of time and existence; and being cosmic means it is fundamentally nothing. In focusing on it you are perceiving both the nothing and the everything simultaneously. The preparation we've been through in the previous four steps provides the accelerated intelligence necessary for this. But you must not doubt. You must not allow your mind or self to judge the situation. Just be. Then focus, and keep doing.

The biological cell is said to be the basic unit of life.

As biology is concerned only with physical effects, what the statement means to say is that the biological cell is the basic unit of all living things, living forms. Of life itself, no explanation is offered or can be offered because appreciation of the reality of the solar plexus depends on self-knowledge, not on the study of things external.

The solar plexus, as the ethereal model of the biological cell, is round in shape with a substantive perimeter and a hole in the middle representing indefinable Life. It resembles what most of the world would call a Lifesaver or Polo Mint – the sweet or candy with a hole.

Please know that this is not visualisation. What I'm attempting to describe is there now, an ethereal reality in your consciousness. The hole in the middle, the nothing, the nucleus, is the revivifying life in your consciousness. The substantive perimeter is the mind, the matter, the world.

In the biological cell the life-centre consists of nucleic acids, DNA or the genetic code. Always moving outwards, DNA carries the essential character of the organism from generation to generation. Similarly, in the cosmic cell, the vibrant life-centre carries outwards the essential self-knowledge of the individual from living life to living life.

The nucleus of every biological cell is said to be fifty per cent water. As water is the substantive symbol of life on earth, it's not surprising that life, both biological and cosmic, flows from the inner to the outer.

So start now by being still and focusing on the solar plexus under the breastplate in the body.

Focus until all sensation stops.

Sensation is the substantive outer perimeter, the matter of existence. It may vanish and then return.

In between is the nothing.

But you can't know the nothing.

Just keep focused.

Don't be in a hurry.

Let whatever happens happen.

Don't force anything.

Don't pull back.

Don't doubt.

Stay with the nothing. It will spread out through the whole body. And you will be nothing and know nothing.

But this nothing is not nothing as the mind conceives nothing. This nothing we're speaking of is the potent source of everything, every thing that you love, treasure and profoundly wish for. Once this nothing is sufficiently entered or realised, a great peace that truly exceeds all understanding naturally descends.

The mind's concept of nothing derives from its assumed fear of extinction at physical death. But at death, with the intelligence freed of the weighty baggage of sensory existence, the mind is automatically transformed into pure unmoving consciousness – the nothing we're speaking of. In other words, entry into the solar plexus is a kind of preview of the wonder and mystery behind death. In this state you are literally 'out of your mind' and behind the physical brain – for death is demonstrably only the death of the flesh and blood brain.

A reminder. In this exercise you are entering the world of knowledge by gradually giving up dependence on knowing. Knowing is of the mind and memory and requires the delay of interpretive thinking and reasoning. Knowledge is instantaneous communication, utterly fulfilling and informing without words or concepts.

Keep doing. It takes practice, lots of practice. The practice is to overcome any impatience or frustration. Your mind and emotions have to stay out of this. Only accelerating intelligence has the swiftness to succeed.

If you have to, break off and start again. But first take two or three deep breaths into the diaphragm or lower belly, holding the intake for a couple of seconds before releasing. This is all part of the exercise. You are actually focusing on, or in a way entering, another dimension which generates a subtle strain. As always, break any momentum by pausing, and then resume from the start.

While focused on any of the body parts or areas we've covered, the sounds of nature and the world will try to make you think by pulling you back into the region between the earth and the moon. This is a test of one-pointedness, of not being distracted from what you are consciously doing.

Also, I have to remind you of an earlier caution. While you're still attached to your prisoners, those emotions in the chest as well as others from the seat of the self in the belly, may creep over the solar plexus and create a false impression that it is vibrating. So for a time you may have a sense of pure sensation in the solar plexus. This is not 'wrong' for pure sensation is of the whole body. But eventually the pure sensation vanishes, the solar plexus starts to open up to your intelligent gaze, and you are in the nothing.

At a recent seminar I used an analogy to illustrate entry into the vastness of the solar plexus, and it may be helpful to repeat it here.

I said, say you're in a big hessian bag, representing your physical body and its world. It's cosy and pretty dark in there but you can breathe quite easily and you're not uncomfortable. One day, you put your head out and see there's an amazingly big new world of sky and light all around. Entranced by the unsuspected freedom and vastness of it all, you keep moving until you're out of the bag. You are now that freedom and vastness. You are no longer apart from it or even a part of it – you are it! You're not concerned about the bag anymore. It's still there, but you don't worry about it like you used to.

You're detached from the body but still in the body. You can still feel the pain of someone standing on your toe but all anxiety has left you. You're in a different place. You haven't left your body in any way – it's just that you're detached from attachment to it!

In practising the spiritual art of meditation there are two opposing dynamics. One is force, the other is power.

Force is the momentum of the mind expressed as thought, emotion, decisions, choices and personal action; in short, human nature. Force is the dynamic responsible for our often violent topsy-turvy world. The violence in human nature is a repeat of the pattern of violence so often encountered in nature, the difference however being that nature, a higher octave of psyche, is free of personal intentions.

The presence of force disturbs the stillness necessary for entry into the solar plexus – and for the realisation of God or Self. However, in practising spiritual meditation you must be careful not to take a forceful or thoughtful role by assuming you are not still enough, or that you can't do it. This is not an area for analysis, decisions or assumptions – or to be looking for something. The answer lies in simply doing it – and seeing the result.

Simply 'doing it' is an example of power. You manifest power by negation – in this case by negating the force of the mind that wants to reflect or consider, instead of simply doing. In any uncertain situation, action will solve the uncertainty. This doesn't mean the solution will please the person; only that that particular uncertainty is solved.

(Chances are that if the person is not pleased with the result, the search for a pleasing solution will continue in the form of more personal or forceful action until either the will, the desire or the money, is exhausted. Better at an earlier stage to have seen the futility of pursuing a wilful course – and to have negated the will or desire, and saved the money!)

Power does not move. Power is the intelligence looking through your senses at this moment. Any reaction or interpretation is movement and that's the mind. That which observes is more powerful than anything observed. Take the phenomenon of kundalini which you may encounter at some stage in meditation. Kundalini is a very refined energy. It rises up without warning from the sacrum area at the base of the spine, straightens the body like a poker, throws the head back, and turns the eyeballs upward 'into' the forehead accompanied by an unemotional release of tears – the whole impulse lasting only a few seconds. Kundalini, although a fine motivating energy, is still a force. Its purpose is to clear inferior obstructions of energy in the spinal column thus allowing a freer flow of consciousness. In Hindu thought kundalini is conceived of as a most desirable and favourable cosmic energy, the word 'cosmic' distinguishing it from the usual unconscious movement of force in the world.

DISCOVER IT FOR YOURSELF

I can't tell where this Fifth Step leads for you except to say it's an opening to solar consciousness or cosmic intelligence. What that means you have to discover for yourself. But I can tell you it works – and that it has worked for others who have diligently practised this meditation.

Here's an excerpt from a Finnish woman's letter:

'The opening in the solar plexus that you've spoken about happened. It was like the back side of my body opened pitch black – my solar plexus as the top of the pyramid-shape opening, and I noticed that at first I did not dare to let go of my body and I got nauseous. But gradually I let go of the whole of my body. First it was moving at incredible speed. Then it was absolutely still, pristine stillness.'

A man from Holland wrote:

'I was sitting with my eyes closed and saw the image

of a sink appearing. Then I became aware of the drain in the middle of it, looked in it and noticed how totally black the hole was. It reminded me of the plexus solaris and next I suddenly went through it and on the other side was ejected for a brief moment into what I experienced as outer space, the solar system (beyond the earth and moon). I was floating in a vast nothingness, empty space, but me being conscious of it. It was wonderful, sweet, cool, lovely, beautiful and free from everything. I wasn't aware of any stars or the sun at that moment, only blackness (although later I felt as if the sun, earth and moon were behind me). Being there lasted only a brief moment but that was enough to experience it.'

A few months later, the same man wrote:

'I was reading one of your catalogues and realised why I had been attracted to your teaching. Suddenly, I became aware of the spirit. It was all around in the room and also in me. The whole scene in front of me became very still, as if time was slowing down and I was looking from a distance at it. Then I looked into my plexus solaris and for the first time I was very aware of the big hole in my body there. Completely empty. The plexus solaris is really a life saver! The whole scene, the whole world, is moving around it as an enormous void. The plexus solaris is the centre of it all, the axle of the wheel, completely still and being nothing. However very powerful, holding everything together, or projecting it out. In the same moment I also became very aware of my mother-in-law who died a couple of weeks before. She was so near and tangible. I almost could touch her, which actually I did, sensing her. She is her essence now, pure love. Silent tears of joy filled my eyes, because of this incredible truth and wonder. Life and death becoming one.'

SEE ALSO

START MEDITATING NOW
Audiobook written and spoken by Barry Long. Listen as he leads you through the first steps of right meditation. It's in two parts. The second contains ten lessons on how to stop thinking.

STILLNESS IS THE WAY
Read this detailed account of a 'meditation intensive' as Barry Long works with seven people over a long weekend. The book includes teachings on very many aspects of the spiritual life.

MEDITATION - A FOUNDATION COURSE
A concise guide to right meditation. This ia a book of ten lessons, with straightforward instruction and sets of exercises to apply in everyday life.

BARRY LONG TEACHINGS
Get books and audiobooks from our online stores and specialist bookshops. There is a Barry Long YouTube Channel and a Barry Long Podcast. Please visit the website of The Barry Long Foundation International.

www.barrylong.org